George Washington's Rules of Civility & Decent Behavior

George Washington's Rules of Civility & Decent Behavior

George Washington

ROWMAN & LITTLEFIELD PUBLISHERS, INC.
Lanham • Boulder • New York • Toronto • Plymouth, UK

Published by Rowman & Littlefield Publishers, Inc.
A wholly owned subsidiary of The Rowman & Littlefield Publishing Group, Inc.
4501 Forbes Boulevard, Suite 200, Lanham, Maryland 20706
www.rowman.com

10 Thornbury Road, Plymouth PL6 7PP, United Kingdom

Distributed by National Book Network

George Washington's Rules of Civility and Decent Behavior was originally published in the late eighteenth century.

Library of Congress Cataloging-in-Publication Data

ISBN: 978-1-4422-2231-1 (cloth : alk. paper)
ISBN: 978-1-4422-2232-8 (electronic)

♾™ The paper used in this publication meets the minimum requirements of American National Standard for Information Sciences—Permanence of Paper for Printed Library Materials, ANSI/NISO Z39.48-1992.

Printed in Malaysia

22nd: Show not yourself glad at the misfortune
of another, though he were your enemy.

—from *George Washington's Rules of Civility & Decent Behavior*

Courtesy of the Library of Congress

WASHINGTON'S
RULES
OF
CIVILITY
&
DECENT
BEHAVIOUR

George Washington, the father of our country, exhibited notable manners throughout his life. Diligence in social matters was common practice in decent society the world over, during his lifetime. At the age of 14, George Washington wrote down 110 rules under the title "Rules of Civility & Decent Behaviour in Company and Conversation." These rules were drawn from an English translation of a French book of maxims and were intended to polish manners, keep alive the best affections of the heart, impress the obligation of moral virtues, teach how to treat others in social relations, and above all, inculcate the practice of a perfect self-control.

WASHINGTON'S
RULES OF CIVILITY & DECENT BEHAVIOUR

1st EVERY action done in company ought to be with some sign of respect to those that are present.

2nd WHEN in company, put not your hands to any part of the body, not usually discovered.

3rd SHOW nothing to your friend that may affright him.

4th IN the presence of others sing not to yourself with a humming noise, nor drum with your fingers or feet.

5th IF you cough, sneeze, sigh, or yawn, do it not loud but privately; and speak not in your yawning, but put your handkerchief or hand before your face and turn aside.

6th S<small>LEEP</small> not when others speak, sit not when others stand, speak not when you should hold your peace, walk not on when others stop.

7th P<small>UT</small> not off your clothes in the presence of others, nor go out your chamber half dressed.

8th A<small>T</small> play and at fire it is good manners to give place to the last comer, and affect not to speak louder than ordinary.

9th S<small>PIT</small> not in the fire, nor stoop low before it. Neither put your hands into the flames to warm them, nor set your feet upon the fire, especially if there be meat before it.

10th W<small>HEN</small> you sit down, keep your feet firm and even, without putting one on the other or crossing them.

11th S<small>HIFT</small> not yourself in the sight of others nor gnaw your nails.

12th SHAKE not the head, feet, or legs; roll not the eyes; lift not one eyebrow higher than the other; wry not the mouth; and bedew no man's face with your spittle by approaching too near him when you speak.

13th KILL no vermin as fleas, lice, ticks &c in the sight of others; if you see any filth or thick spittle, put your foot dexteriously upon it; if it be upon the clothes of your companions, put it off privately; and if it be upon your own clothes, return thanks to him who puts it off.

14th TURN not your back to others especially in speaking; jog not the table or desk on which another reads or writes; lean not upon any one.

15th KEEP your nails clean and short, also your hands and teeth clean, yet without showing any great concern for them.

16th DO not puff up the cheeks; loll not out the tongue, rub the hands, or beard, thrust out the lips, or bite them, or keep the lips too open or close.

17th BE no flatterer; neither play with any that delights not to be played with.

18th READ no letters, books, or papers in company; but when there is a necessity for the doing of it, you must ask leave. Come not near the books or writings of another so as to read them or give your opinion of them unasked; also look not nigh when another is writing a letter.

19th LET your countenance be pleasant, but in serious matters somewhat grave.

20th THE gestures of the body must be suited to the discourse you are upon.

21st REPROACH none for the infirmities of nature, nor delight to put them that have in mind thereof.

22nd SHOW not yourself glad at the misfortune of another, though he were your enemy.

23rd WHEN you see a crime punished, you may be inwardly pleased, but always show pity to the suffering offender.

24th DO not laugh too much or too loud in public.

25th SUPERFLUOUS compliments and all affectation of ceremony are to be avoided, yet where due, they are not to be neglected.

26th IN pulling off your hat to persons of distinction, as noblemen, justices, churchmen, &c, make a reverence, bowing more or less according to the custom of the better bred and quality of the person. Among your equals, expect not always that they should begin with you first, but to pull off your hat when there is no need is affectation; in the matter of saluting and resaluting in words, keep to the most usual custom.

27ᵗʰ Tɪs ill manners to bid one more eminent than yourself be covered as well as not to do it to whom it's due; likewise, he that makes too much haste to put on his hat does not well, yet he ought to put it on at the first, or at most the second time of being asked. Now what is herein spoken, of qualification in behavior in saluting, ought to be observed in taking of place, and sitting down for ceremonies without bounds is troublesome.

28ᵗʰ Iꜰ anyone come to speak to you while you are sitting, stand up, though he be your inferior; and when you present seats, let it be to everyone according to his degree.

29ᵗʰ Wʜᴇɴ you meet with one of greater quality than yourself, stop, and retire, especially if it be a door or any straight place to give way for him to pass.

30ᵗʰ Iɴ walking, the highest place in most countries seems to be on the right hand, therefore, place yourself on the left of him whom you desire to honour; but if three walk together, the mid place is the most honourable; the wall is usually given to the most worthy if two walk together.

31st If any one far surpasses others, either in age, estate, or merit, yet would give place to one meaner than himself in his own lodging, the one ought not to accept it; so he, on the other hand, should not use much earnestness nor offer it above once or twice.

32nd To one that is your equal, or not much inferior, you are to give the chief place in your lodging; and he to who it is offered ought at the first to refuse it, but at the second to accept, though not without acknowledging his own unworthiness.

33rd They that are in dignity or in office have in all places precedency; but whilst they are young, they ought to respect those that are their equals in birth or other qualities, though they have no public charge.

34ᵗʰ   Iᴛ is good manners to prefer them to whom we speak before ourselves, especially if they be above us with whom in no sort we ought to begin.

35ᵗʰ   Lᴇᴛ your discourse with men of business be short and comprehensive.

36ᵗʰ   Aʀᴛɪꜰɪᴄᴇʀs & persons of low degree ought not to use many ceremonies to Lords or others of high degree, but respect and highly honor them; and those of high degree ought to treat them with affability & courtesy, without arrogance.

37ᵗʰ   Iɴ speaking to men of quality, do not lean nor look them full in the face, nor approach too near them, at least keep a full pace from them.

38ᵗʰ   Iɴ visiting the sick, do not presently play the physician if you be not knowing therein.

39th IN writing or speaking, give every person his due title according to his degree & the custom of the place.

40th STRIVE not with your superiors in argument, but always submit your judgment to others with modesty.

41st UNDERTAKE not to teach your equal in the art himself professes, it savours of arrogance.

42nd LET thy ceremonies in courtesy be proper to the dignity of his place with who thou converses, for it is absurd to act the same with a clown and a prince.

43rd DO not express joy before one sick or in pain, for that contrary passion will aggravate his misery.

44th WHEN a man does all he can though it succeeds not well blame not him that did it.

45th   B<small>EING</small> to advise or reprehend any one, consider whether it ought to be in public or private, presently or at some other time, in what terms to do it; and in reproving show no sign of cholar, but do it with all sweetness and mildness.

46th   T<small>AKE</small> all admonitions thankfully in what time or place soever given, but afterwards, not being culpable, take a time & place convenient to let him know it that gave them.

47th   M<small>OCK</small> not nor jest at any thing of importance; break no jests that are sharp biting; and if you deliver any thing witty and pleasant, abstain from laughing thereat yourself.

48th   W<small>HEREIN</small> you reprove another be unblameable yourself, for example is more prevalent than precepts.

49th   U<small>SE</small> no reproachful language against any one; neither curse nor revile.

50th BE not hasty to believe flying reports to the disparagement of any.

51st WEAR not your clothes foul, ripped or dusty, but see that they be brushed once every day, at least, and take heed that you approach not to any uncleaness.

52nd IN your apparel be modest and endeavour to accomodate nature; rather than to procure admiration, keep to the fashion of your equals, such as are civil and orderly with respect to times and places.

53rd RUN not in the streets; neither go too slowly nor with mouth open; go not shaking your arms; kick not the earth with your feet; go not upon the toes nor in a dancing fashion.

54th PLAY not the peacock, looking everywhere about you, to see if you be well decked, if your shoes fit well, if your stockings sit neatly, and clothes handsomely.

55th Eat not in the streets nor in the house out of season.

56th Associate yourself with men of good quality, if you esteem your own reputation; for it is better to be alone than in bad company.

57th In walking up and down in a house, only with one in company if he be greater than yourself, at the first give him the right hand and stop not till he does and be not the first that turns; and when you do turn let it be with your face towards him; if he be a man of great quality, walk not with him cheek by joul, but somewhat behind him, but yet in such a manner that he may easily speak to you.

58th Let your conversation be without malice or envy, for it is a sign of a tractable and commendable nature; and in all cases of passion admit reason to govern.

59th   Never express anything unbecoming nor act against the rules moral before your inferiors.

60th   Be not immodest in urging your friends to discover a secret.

61st   Utter not base and frivilous things amongst grave and learned men; nor very difficult questions or subjects among the ignorant; or with things hard to be believed, stuff not your discourse with sentences, amongst your betters nor equals.

62nd   Speak not of doleful things in a time of mirth or at the table; speak not of melancholy things as death and wounds, and if others mention them, change if you can the discourse. Tell not your dreams, but to your intimate friend.

63rd   A man ought not to value himself of his achievements or rare qualities of wit, much less of his riches, virtue or kindred.

64th　 Break not a jest where none take pleasure in mirth; laugh not aloud, nor at all without occasion; deride no man's misfortune, though there seems to be some cause.

65th　 Speak not injurious words, neither in jest or earnest; scoff at none although they give occasion.

66th　 Be not forward but friendly and courteous; be the first to salute, hear, and answer; & be not pensive when it's time to converse.

67th　 Detract not from others; neither be excessive in commanding.

68th　 Go not thither, where you know not, whether you shall be welcome or not. Give not advice without being asked & when desired do it briefly.

69th　 If two contend together, take not the part of either unconstrained; and be not obstinate in your own opinion; in things indifferent be of the major side.

70th REPREHEND not the imperfections of others, for that belongs to parents, masters, and superiors.

71st GAZE not on the marks or blemishes of others and ask not how they came. What you may speak in secret to your friend, deliver not before others.

72nd SPEAK not in an unknown tongue in company, but in your own language and that as those of quality do and not as the vulgar. Sublime matters treat seriously.

73rd THINK before you speak; pronounce not imperfectly nor bring out your words too hastily, but orderly & distinctly.

74th WHEN another speaks be attentive yourself and disturb not the audience; if any hesitates in his words, help him not, nor prompt him without desired; interrupt him not, nor answer him till his speech be ended.

75th IN the midst of discourse ask not of what one treateth, but if you perceive any stop because of your coming you may well intreat him gently to proceed. If a person of quality comes in while you are conversing, it is handsome to repeat what was said before.

76th WHILE you are talking, point not with your finger at him of whom you discourse nor approach too near him to whom you talk, especially to his face.

77th TREAT with men at fit times about business; and whisper not in the company of others.

78th MAKE no comparisons; and if any of the company be commended for any brave act of virtue, commend not another for the same.

79th B<small>E</small> not apt to relate news if you know not the truth thereof. In discoursing of things you have heard, name not your author; always a secret discover not.

80th B<small>E</small> not tedious in discourse or in reading unless you find the company pleased therewith.

81st B<small>E</small> not curious to know the affairs of others; neither approach those that speak in private.

82nd U<small>NDERTAKE</small> not what you cannot perform, but be careful to keep your promise.

83rd W<small>HEN</small> you deliver a matter do it with passion & with discretion, however mean the person be you do it to.

84th W<small>HEN</small> your superiors talk to any body, hearken not neither speak nor laugh.

85th In company of those of higher quality than yourself, speak not until you are asked a question, then stand upright, put of your hat, & answer in few words.

86th In disputes, be not so desirous to overcome as not to give liberty to each one to deliver his opinion and submit to the judgment of the major part, especially if they are judges of the dispute.

87th Let thy carriage be such as becomes a man: grave, settled, and attentive to that which is spoken. Contradict not at every turn what others say.

88th Be not tedious in discourse, make not many digressions, nor repeat often the same manner of discourse.

89th Speak not evil of the absent, for it is unjust.

90th Being set at meat, scratch not; neither spit,

cough, or blow your nose, except if there is a necessity for it.

91st MAKE no show of taking great delight in your victuals; feed not with greediness; cut your bread with a knife; lean not on the table; neither find fault with what you eat.

92nd TAKE no salt, nor cut your bread with your knife greasy.

93rd ENTERTAINING anyone at the table it is decent to present him with meat; undertake not to help others undesired by the master.

94th IF you soak your bread in the sauce, let it be no more than what you put in your mouth at a time; and blow not your broth at table but stay till it cools of itself.

95th PUT not your meat to your mouth with your knife in your hand; neither spit forth the stones of any fruit pie upon a dish nor cast anything under the table.

96th IT is unbecoming to stoop too much to one's meat. Keep your fingers clean & when foul, wipe them on a corner of your table napkin.

97th PUT not another bit into your mouth till the former be swallowed. Let not your morsels be too big.

98th DRINK not, nor talk with your mouth full; neither gaze about you while you are drinking.

99th DRINK not too leisurely, nor yet too hastily; before and after drinking, wipe your lips; breath not then or ever with too great a noise, for it is uncivil.

100th CLEANSE not your teeth with the table cloth napkin, fork, or knife; but if others do it, let it be done with a pick tooth.

101st RINSE not your mouth in the presence of others.

102nd I<small>T</small> is out of use to call upon the company often to eat; nor need you drink to others every time you drink.

103rd I<small>N</small> company of your betters, be not longer in eating than they are; lay not your arm but only your hand upon the table.

104th I<small>T</small> belongs to the chiefest in company to unfold his napkin and fall to meat first, but he ought then to begin in time & to dispatch with dexterity that the slowest may have time allowed him.

105th B<small>E</small> not angry at table whatever happens, and if you have reason to be so, show it not; put on a cheerful countenance especially if there be strangers, for good humour makes one dish of meat a feast.

106th S<small>ET</small> not yourself at the upper end of the table; but if it be your due or that the master of the house would have it so, contend not, least you should trouble the company.

107th IF others talk at the table, be attentive; but talk not with meat in your mouth.

108th WHEN you speak of God or his attributes, let it be seriously & with reverence. Honour & obey your natural parents although they be poor.

109th LET your recreations be manful not sinful.

110th LABOUR to keep alive in your breast that little celestial fire called conscience.